# FROM BR TO BEECHING

## VOLUME ONE

# The Routes of t[he] Castles and [Kings]

by PATRICK WHITEHOUSE and DAVID JENKINSON

FRONT COVER
Castle Class 4-6-0 No. 7005 *Sir Edward Elgar*
awaits departure from Hereford Station.
(P. M. Alexander/Millbrook House Collection)

REAR COVER
Star Class 4-6-0 No. 4062 *Malmesbury Abbey*
near Thingley Junction with the 4.07 pm
Swindon to Bristol train.
(P. M. Alexander/Millbrook House Collection)

Close-up of the nameplate of Castle Class
No. 5081 *Lockheed Hudson*
(P. M. Alexander/Millbrook House Collection)

ISBN 0-906899-40-0

FIRST PUBLISHED 1990

PHOTOGRAPHS:
As credited.

DESIGNED BY
BARNABUS DESIGN & PRINT · TRURO · CORNWALL
TYPESET BY
TYPESTYLE · TRURO · CORNWALL
PRINTED BY
CENTURY LITHO · PENRYN · CORNWALL
BOUND BY
BOOTHS BOOKBINDERS · PENRYN · CORNWALL
PUBLISHED BY
ATLANTIC TRANSPORT PUBLISHERS
TREVITHICK HOUSE · WEST END
PENRYN · CORNWALL TR10 8HE

# CONTENTS

In offering this new series of books to our readers, it occurred to us that a few preliminary words in this first volume would not be out of place regarding the reasons for the compilation of the whole series. Firstly, of course, we both like to share our knowledge of railway history with others and are, happily, in a position to be able to do so in tangible form. But the overriding reason for compiling this series was our feeling that the demise of the steam railway in the form we both knew it, was truly the end of an era and that there were many signs that some very strange ideas were beginning to develop about how and why the steam railway worked as it did. We felt that we were in a position to do something about it.

This is not to decry the efforts of the preservation movement – the only way in which the modern devotee can experience live steam and an area in which both of us, in different ways, have been actively involved for many years. But, try though they might (and some do so very hard indeed), the preserved railways can never fully re-create the historical reality; it will always have an air of artificiality about it. We no longer use rail transport in its traditional mode and though often perfectly relevant to the changed circumstances of our own day and age, the preserved lines can never really put the clock back. But properly interpreted historical railway photographs can – hence these books.

One of the more startling facts to note is that the basic method of operating a steam railway hardly changed in essence from the beginning of the century to the end of steam itself. True, the hardware changed at regular intervals but the basic *modus operandi* of the 1950s and early 1960s would have been perfectly intelligible to a late Victorian time-traveller were such a person to have existed. But the end of the steam railway also coincided with a great upsurge in railway photography which meant that most of the traditional methodology was eventually and accurately recorded on film. This explosion of activity was at its height in the immediate post- nationalisation period, hence our choice of title and historical period for the series.

Our aim, therefore, has been to use this rich vein of illustrative material to put on record some of the many facets of railway operation which died for ever after the mid-1960s. It is not meant to be a deep and comprehensive railway history, nor will every corner of the kingdom be covered – indeed there may well be some yawning gaps. But we do hope that as the series builds up, we shall be able to present a simple but accurate summation, using pictures from its final years, not only of the last phase of the pure steam railway itself but also the fundamental way in which it had been operated for 70 years or maybe more. We have also made a conscious endeavour to locate as many unpublished views as possible.

We have naturally drawn on our own knowledge and experience in assembling these books but since we would never claim to have more than partial knowledge in many areas, the total compilation has also been very much a team job. No one can or should even try to rely solely on his own memory or knowledge so a consultancy panel comprising John Edgington of the National Railway Museum and John Smart of Millbrook House has spent many hours alongside the authors trying to get it right. We are especially grateful to them for this – it makes such a difference.

Reference has also been made to a number of specialist publications as well as to the numerous magazines available. Those relevant to any specific volume are listed in a short Bibliography at the end of each book.

**Patrick Whitehouse**          **David Jenkinson**

# THE STARS, CASTLES AND KINGS

Star by name and Star by nature; Churchward's four cylinder 4-6-0s built between 1905 and 1923 were not only pioneers in their own right, but also represented the zenith of English express locomotive practice up to the time of Grouping. The last batch led directly to the Castle class of 1923, itself the harbinger of the Kings of 1927, the most powerful 4-6-0s ever to run in Great Britain.

The Stars were one of the results of experiments and trials conducted by G. J. Churchward using three 4-cylinder French compound Atlantics, 2-cylinder 4-6-0s and 4-4-2s (later rebuilt to 4-6-0s) plus a 4-cylinder simple 4-4-2 also rebuilt as a 4-6-0. The end products became the famous 2-cylinder Saints and 4-cylinder Stars; in tandem the two classes were the principal Great Western express classes until superseded by the more advanced Collett Castles and Kings. All in all there were 73 Stars. In spite of the fact that the GW/BR built 171 Castles (including conversions) the '29s' and 'Small 40s', as the Saints and Stars were also known, lasted until well into the BR era. Eventually displaced on the West of England and Birmingham expresses by their more modern sisters, the Stars continued to work heavy trains including the North to West expresses and often the Birkenhead-Bournemouths and Birkenhead-Margates between Shrewsbury and Oxford. By the time covered by this book they were largely relegated to semi-fast or parcels trains; but even then the Stars were still occasionally called upon – right to the end – to work heavy reliefs and gave excellent accounts of themselves.

Churchward had originally proposed to enlarge the Star design by using the boiler off the big 47XX fast freight class 2-8-0 but this was deemed to be too heavy and the Stars were modernised into the Castles by a compromise using the new Swindon No. 8 boiler. Even so when the first of these came out (No. 4073 Caerphilly Castle), it was the most powerful engine in the country. The main difference to the outside world was the provision of an enlarged side-window cab. Originally the Castles had the then-standard 3500 gallon tenders but these were later changed to the new 4000 gallon type; some Stars were later fitted with 4000 gallon tenders as well. The building of Castles continued until 1950 – including early rebuilds of Stars and the ten later Abbeys plus the reconstructed No. 111, originally the solitary GWR Pacific Great Bear.

After World War II, the new Castles all had three (in lieu of two) row superheaters and mechanical lubricators. After the poor showing of the Kings in the 1948 Trials and their general modification using four row superheaters and double chimneys these features also began to appear on the Castles as they passed through Swindon works after 1956. For more than thirty years the Castles were the supreme motive power for all but the heaviest West of England and Birmingham expresses and had a profound effect on the express engine design of other companies during the inter-war years. Like the Stars, the Castles were 'Red Route' engines which classification encompassed most of the main lines of the old GWR. During the period covered by this book they could be seen on virtually all the principal routes of the Western Region.

As the Castles were not as big as the traffic department might have wished during the early 1920s, some hard talking must have been done for by 1926, the GWR civil engineer had completed a heavy bridge strengthening programme on the West of England and Birmingham main lines allowing a well balanced 22.5 ton axle loading.

The Kings were built in 1927 to take full advantage of this; but it was many years before any other routes became suitable for this 'Double Red' class, one of only thirty members.

The Kings were constructed in a railway era of competitiveness and in order to claim them as being 'the most powerful in Britain' (on a tractive effort basis) the GWR tacked a quarter of an inch onto the cylinder diameters and reduced the driving wheel size slightly from 6ft 9in to 6ft 6in!* The most obvious outward changes from the Churchward design were the fat No. 12 boiler and the bogie. To keep this clear of the cylinders with adequate clearances on curves it was built with outside bearings for the leading axle. Even so the main frame had to have the 'dishing' introduced with the Castles.

The Kings and Castles (but not the Stars) shared the experiments with liveries during early BR days. Of the Kings, Nos. 6001, 6009, 6025 and 6026 all became dark ultramarine blue with LNWR-style red, cream and grey lining. Later, along with all the other members of the class, they received the BR 'Principal Express Passenger' livery – a somewhat lighter shade of blue with black and white lining. This shade too was abandoned in 1951-2 (it did not, apparently, wear too well) and they reverted to the almost GWR shade of green, with orange and black lining, which had already been adopted from 1949 onwards for all 'Secondary' express types, including the Stars and Castles.

The livery experiments on the Castles began with Nos. 7010-3, outshopped from Swindon when a new in 1948 in experimental light apple green (more or less the LNER shade) with LNWR style lining. Nos. 4089, 4091, 5010, 5021 and 5023 were also repainted in like style, but in due course, BR green became the customary livery for the Castles from 1949 onwards. We shall not get drawn into the argument as to whether this BR green was identical to the old GWR shade. We believe that it was *meant* to be so (just as the 1956 shade of BR maroon was officially intended to match the old LMS crimson lake colour), but there would undoubtedly be slight changes of hue between paint batches, or even between the shades offered by the different paint manufacturers.

As has been mentioned earlier, the King class, represented by No. 6018 *King Henry VI,* did not distinguish itself in the 1948 trials, but the

**Above:** *A close up of Star class No. 4022 (6/09-2/52) once* King William, *renamed* The Belgian Monarch (*later* Belgian Monarch) *on the advent of the Kings, but finally rendered anonymous in May 1940 when it was felt that the Belgian King had let the side down over the German invasion of the Low Countries. The words 'Star Class' were painted over the centre splasher. The photograph also shows the lack of splasher beading – removed during the 1914-18 war from Nos. 4000-60; it was never replaced except on some engines rebuilt as* Castles. *The speed recording apparatus and bracket over the rear rhs driver is also apparent. The GWR green lined livery is clearly shown although the full words "BRITISH RAILWAYS" appear on the tender. As the photograph was taken in 1948 the repaint job would also have been in the old GWR colours as the new BR green livery had not yet been adopted. Note the reversing handle sticking well out into the cab. No. 4022 was a Swindon engine throughout its BR ownership. (M. W. Earley Collection-NRM)*

rebuilding with a four-row superheater and double chimney (all members of the class were converted) effected a considerable improvement to the subsequent performance. In BR days, the 'Double Red' routes were extended to cover Filton Junction and Stoke Gifford – Severn Tunnel – Cardiff, Newport – Pontypool Road – Shrewsbury and Wolverhampton – Shrewsbury – Chester.

The Stars, Castles and Kings died hard. The new Castles killed off the remaining Stars and the diesel-hydraulics on the West of England and Birmingham routes did the same to the Kings. The Castles lingered on for a few more years, their last scheduled express turn being the route of the Cathedrals Express: Paddington – Oxford – Worcester –

Hereford. But even the Castles were seen off eventually and the very last one of all, No. 7029 *Clun Castle,* was withdrawn from Gloucester Horton Road depot on 31st December 1965.

*NOTE: Nominal tractive effort is only one method of stating locomotive power, being a theoretical calculation based on boiler pressure, cylinder size and driving wheel diameter. It took no account of thermodynamic efficiency and in later years, generated horsepower (at the cylinders or drawbar) came to be regarded as a more accurate measure of power. This could (and did) result in many cases where engines with lower tractive effort could deliver more horsepower than those which were theoretically 'more powerful'. But in the 1920s, tractive effort was the measure by which railways usually made their comparisons.

**Above:** *No. 4083 Abbotsbury Castle (5/25-12/61) of Stafford Road shed (84A) is prepared, on the middle road at Bath Spa station, prior to taking a stopping train to Swindon. The driver is oiling round without having taken the precaution of putting the locomotive exactly into mid-gear. Bath was a restricted station site so a number of space saving features were used. Access to the sidings in the foreground was via a small wagon turntable whilst Bath passenger signal box above the station roof also had the advantage of giving excellent visibility on the curve through the station. No. 4083 is in the early BR green livery – ie with the first style of tender emblem. (P.M. Alexander/Millbrook House Collection)*

**Above:** *Portrait of a King. By the water column adjacent to the turntable at Stafford Road shed No. 6000 King George V has been coaled up and is ready for the road on 30th September 1961. By now, the Kings had received new double chimneys and four-row super-heaters, the former very obvious and the latter revealed by the much larger casing between chimney and handrail at the boiler/smokebox junction. The commemorative American bell (fitted to the locomotive to mark its 1927 visit to the USA) still adorns the front buffer plank and the engine carries its final BR livery with the second pattern of tender emblem. (K. Cooper/Millbrook House Collection)*

## NOTE ON GWR ROUTE RESTRICTIONS

The Stars and Castles had a red route restriction code – ie routes permitted to all engines with a maximum axle load over 17 tons 12 cwts. The Kings however were given their own double red restriction as their axle load was 22 tons 10 cwts. The original double red routes were as follows:

Paddington-Devonport via Bristol and via
the Westbury route.
Wootton Bassett-Bristol via Badminton.
Paddington-Wolverhampton via Bicester.
Newton Abbot-Kingswear.
Plymouth North Road Junction-Millbay
(for the docks); but at 20 mph maximum.
Bristol relief lines.

The Weston-super-Mare loop, at 20 mph,
maximum.

British Railways extended the double red routes to include:

Stoke Gifford and Filton Junctions-Cardiff.
Newport Maindee Junction-Shrewsbury.
Wolverhampton-Chester.

The red routes (including double red) comprised the majority of the GWR main lines.

Other than those listed above, there were also dotted red routes over which red restricted engines were permitted to work if their speed did not exceed 20 mph. For example the Whitland-Pembroke Dock line was dotted red between Whitland and Tenby although beyond Tenby the line was ordinary red restriction.

# The West of England Main Line
# Paddington to Penzance via Bristol or Westbury

**Above:** One of Eric Treacy's rare photographs taken on Great Western territory: No. 7006 *Lydford Castle* after arrival at No. 9 platform Paddington, probably with an up Gloucester express, given that the engine was allocated to Horton Road (85B). The date is not known (few if any of Eric Treacy's negatives were listed or dated) but would seem to be in the early 1950s. No. 7006 was the penultimate Great Western-built Castle, completed in 6/46 and withdrawn from Old Oak Common in 12/63. It has the final Hawksworth style tender and is in back gear having 'eased up' for uncoupling in readiness to go down to Ranelagh Bridge for servicing. (Eric Treacy/Millbrook House Collection)

**Above:** Another Paddington arrival, this time at night: No. 5040 *Stokesay Castle* (6/35-10/63), again at Platform 9. The train is the 4.45 pm from Bristol Temple Meads via Bath and it is December 1957 when steam was very much in its Indian Summer. No. 5040 was then an Old Oak Common engine (81A) and is also coupled to the final style of GWR tender. Note too the baulk road and the drainage channel for sleeping cars. These channels were sometimes irreverently referred to as 's . . t gullies', for obvious reasons, it being normal to allow passengers to remain on board the sleeping cars – and use the full sanitary facilities – until c. 7.30 am! (G. F. Heiron)

**Right:** Stafford Road based No. 6011 *King James I* (4/28-12/62) in early BR standard blue livery leaves Paddington in the early 1950s and passes by Ranelagh Bridge, the servicing point for engines needing a quick turn round. Note the coal slacker pipe hanging out from the fireman's side and the Great Western headlamps. The train is almost certainly a down Birmingham (Snow Hill) and Wolverhampton (Low Level) fast with its leading coach an old wooden 1907 brake composite now repanelled. (Eric Treacy/Millbrook House Collection)

**Right:** A winter's day at Reading only one month into Nationalisation. Castle class No. 5076 *Gladiator* (8/38-9/64) comes under the gantry on the through road with a Weston-super-Mare express on 31st January 1948. Originally called *Drysllwyn Castle* the engine was renamed after a famous war plane, one of several thus honoured, as a wartime gesture in January 1941. Both train and engine are remarkably clean for the period; the latter carries the post war livery with G (crest) W on the tender and no lining on the cylinder casings. It was allocated to Bristol Bath Road which became 82A under the BR shed coding scheme, a system of shed identification and classification based on former LMS principles. (P. M. Alexander/Millbrook House Collection)

**Left:** Loco exchange. Swindon station in the early 1950s with the 10.55 am Swansea to Sheffield (via Banbury and Woodford) in the platform. It is a Sunday when there was a long wait from 2.46 to 3.38 pm, probably as recovery time for engineering work which was endemic at the time. The Castle is No. 5084 *Reading Abbey* (12/22-7/62, though officially this was a new engine after 'rebuilding' in April 1937) allocated to Swindon (82C). The LNER-designed B1 is No. 61313 allocated to Sheffield Darnall, complete with electric headlamps – the generator is on the right hand side running plate by the smokebox. (P. M. Alexander/Millbrook House Collection)

**Left:** Just outshopped from the works, No. 5056 *Earl of Powis* (6/36-11/64) stands alongside Wolverhampton built 0-6-0 pannier tank No. 1799 dating from 1895 (originally a saddle tank) at Swindon on 8th October 1950. Its shed plate (81A) shows that it is an Old Oak Common engine. Technically No. 1799 (one of the '1854' class) was withdrawn in 12/49 but, as sometimes the case if the boiler was sound, finished off her life as a works shunter. (P. M. Alexander/Millbrook House Collection)

**Below:** Swindon shed on 30th April 1950 with one of the later Stars to be built, No. 4062 *Malmesbury Abbey* (5/22-11/56), unusually coupled to a later flat-sided Hawksworth tender. It was only recently out of shops, having received elbow steam pipes in March that year, and had been a Swindon engine since Nationalisation. No. 4062 was one of the last three Stars to remain in service; most went in the early 1950s with the building of the extra Castles and then the coming of the Britannias. Note the 'dip' between the engine and tender most likely due to the poor shed track behind the rear coupled wheels — but a comfort to modellers whose engines do not always sit squarely! (P. M. Alexander/Millbrook House Collection)

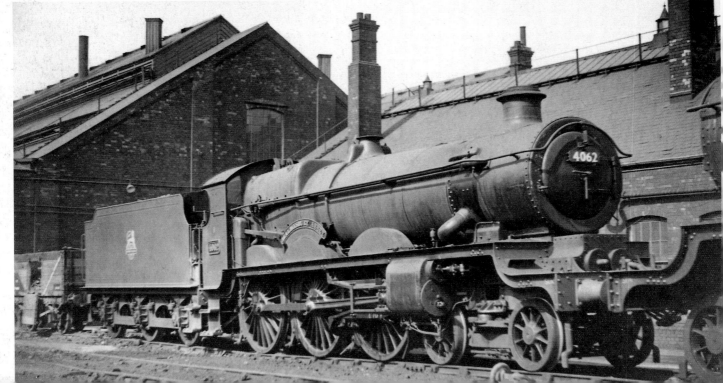

**Right:** The pioneer Star, No. 4000 *North Star* (originally built in 1906 as an Atlantic to compare with the French de Glehn compounds and reconstructed as a 4-6-0 in 1909) in Swindon works in 1954, as a Castle. This was one of the earlier rebuilds – 11/29. Its 'predecessor', the replica broad gauge *North Star* can be seen in the background. Allocated to Stafford Road Wolverhampton (84A), No. 4000 lasted until May 1957 when all her true pedigree sisters had gone, though she was one of the early Castles to be scrapped. The word 'scrap' in chalk on the smokebox door must have related to that component alone. Swindon works closed in March 1986. (M. W. Earley Collection-NRM)

**Right:** Sometime in the summer of 1952, No. 5096 *Bridgwater Castle* (6/39-6/64) approaches Wootton Bassett station, Wilts with a Bristol to Paddington express, its train composed of largely unrepainted GWR stock. Wootton Bassett is the junction for Bath and Bristol on the one hand (the old main line) and the 1903 Badminton cut off on the other. Note the interesting splitting distant signal providing indications of the junction signal ahead – the identical height of the signal arms denoting that both lines have equal status. No. 5096 was then allocated to Bristol Bath Road (82A). (P. M. Alexander/Millbrook House Collection)

**Left:** A King on the 'Bristolian'. No. 6028 *King George VI* (7/30-11/62) heads the down train near Chippenham around 1954 when the 105 minute timing was restored; this was a normal turn for the class during this period. The train is right up to date with a rake of BR Mk I coaches and the engine has now been restored to green livery with the first BR tender emblem. Later the Bristolian was normally Castle-worked with a seven coach formation, but on Fridays the load was increased and a King often substituted. The up train ran via the Badminton cut off. No. 6028 was then an Old Oak Common (81A) engine. (P. M. Alexander/Millbrook House Collection)

**Above:** This fine atmospheric view shows the pioneer Castle No. 4073 *Caerphilly Castle* (8/23-5/60), then allocated to Bristol Bath Road, heading a Bath-Swindon stopping train on 31st January 1953. This 11.23 am service from Bath was a normal 'running in' turn which could often sport a beautifully painted clean and polished Castle or King. No. 4073 now rests in the Science Museum, South Kensington coupled to an original 3500 gallon tender of the type carried when the engine was first built. (P. M. Alexander/Millbrook House Collection)

**Below:** On 14th December 1952 and in the last year of its life, No. 111 *Viscount Churchill*, a Laira (83D) engine, comes up to the 1 in 100 before Middle Hill and Box tunnels (the steepest gradient which Brunel allowed on his main line) with the 7.05 am Plymouth (North Road) to Paddington via Bristol and Bath (SuO). Rebuilt from the legendary 4-6-2 *Great Bear* (the Great Western's one and only Pacific), in September 1924, No. 111 was ostensibly a Castle though using the front portion of the old engine's frames. No. 111 was one of the first Castles to be withdrawn – in July 1953. (P. M. Alexander/Millbrook House Collection)

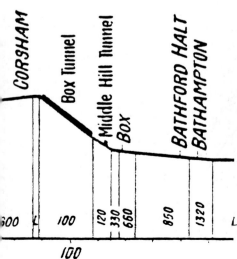

**Opposite:** The first of its class to be built under BR auspices, No. 7008 *Swansea Castle* (5/48-9/64) leaves Box station (closed 4/1/65) with a 'running in' turn – again the 11.23 am from Bath to Swindon service – on 10th October 1952. In addition to providing a pristine engine this train often boasted a fascinating leading vehicle in the form of a Swindon works stores van used for taking parts to the various depots. In this view, a Dean clerestory brake serves duty; it was originally one of two 56ft full brakes (with lavatory), Nos. 1069/70 built in 1897 for the GWR Royal train. In 1932 No. 1069 became a departmental stores van whilst No. 1070 was used by the Hotels and Restaurants Department. No. 7008 was allocated to Oxford (81F) at the time of this picture. (P. M. Alexander/Millbrook House Collection)

**Above:** Still with its lower superheat and taller GWR chimney, burnished 4-6-0 No. 5014 *Goodrich Castle* (6/32-2/65) pulls out of Bath Spa with the down 'Merchant Venturer', a train second only in prestige to the 'Bristolian'. The date is 1952 – some twelve months after the naming of the 11.15 am from Paddington in Festival of Britain year. The train has a mixture of GWR stock, many coaches still with an external door to every compartment. No. 5014 was then allocated to Old Oak Common shed (81A). Note the differing angles of the signal arms – the distant was probably motor worked. (G. F. Heiron)

**Below:** One of the 1914 batch of Stars named after Princesses, No. 4055 *Princess Sophia* (7/14-2/51) leaves Twerton Tunnel, near Bath, with the 4.07 pm Swindon to Bristol passenger and (empty) milk train on 11th September 1950. *Princess Sophia* was then a Swindon engine with but six months to live and has spare headlamps, Great Western fashion, on the running plate. (P. M. Alexander/Millbrook House Collection)

**Above:** Train No. 107, the 12.00 noon to Paddington, pulls out of Bristol Temple Meads behind Castle class No. 5082 *Swordfish* (6/39-7/62) on a summer day in 1953. It has used one of the 'new' platforms built in 1935 using government money to provide employment. The leading coaches are all ex-GWR. Note the very Great Western water tank, with its corrugated iron roof to stop (or rather slow down) corrosion, which seems still to carry its GWR 'livery'. No. 5082 was originally named *Powis Castle* but carried 'Warplane' plates from January 1941. When pictured here, it was an Old Oak Common (81A) engine working its way home. (G. F. Heiron)

**Right:** A blue King (probably with a red-backed nameplate) No. 6002 *King William IV* (7/27-9/62), of Old Oak Common (81A) on Bristol Bath Road shed (82A) in 1950. Note the 20 ton loco coal wagon in the left hand background. This design of steel-bodied 20T wagon with double side doors was very much a feature of the old GWR and great rakes of them could often be seen proceeding from South Wales to all parts of the old GWR system, loaded with their famous 'Welsh Steam Coal', the essential 'diet' for any self-respecting GWR locomotive! The crane (probably for clearing the ash pits) and the water column in the shed yard should also be noted. (P. M. Alexander/Millbrook House Collection)

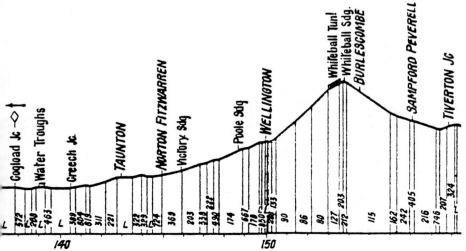

Above: One of the last batch of pre-war built 51XX class 2-6-2 tanks (11/39), No. 4136 of Taunton shed, is one of the day's bankers as No. 5059 *Earl St. Aldwyn* reaches Whiteball summit in fine style with an Exeter to Taunton train on 19th May 1950. The Castle (allocated to Exeter – 83C) still carries its Great Western number on the buffer beam though it has British Railways (in GWR style lettering) on the tender. It was built in May 1937 and withdrawn during the 'mass-murder' period of 1962. The leading coach is a GWR toplight brake third. Note the down refuge siding, complete with catch point. On the up side is a siding for the banking engines, the crossover being just out of picture to the right. The bracket signal controls the entrance to the down relief line (beyond the bridge) which came into use in 1927. (P. M. Alexander/Millbrook House Collection)

**Right:** On the Westbury route at Great Cheverell, Wilts, No. 6008 *King James II* (3/28-6/62), recently fitted with large steam pipes and based at Laira (83D), heads the up 'Cornish Riviera Express' on Sunday 15th March 1953. It is one of the March 1928 batch of Kings and was the last to be fitted with high degree superheat and a double chimney (12/58). This would be the reduced winter formation for the 'Cornish Riviera' composed mostly of post-war Hawksworth stock. (P. M. Alexander/Millbrook House Collection)

**Below:** Yatton at the end of an era: Saturday 7th September 1963, the last day of the summer timetable and consequently the last day of steam on the Paddington to Weston-super-Mare service and for passenger trains over the Cheddar branch. Old Oak Common based No. 7036 *Taunton Castle* (built 8/50) heads the 9.45 am (SO) Paddington-Weston whilst LMS Ivatt 2-6-2T No. 41245 (of Barrow Road, ex Midland, shed; Bath Road having already closed) takes water from the long arm of the platform tank as it waits with the 1.45 pm for Wells; both engines are filthy and the Castle also has a very ersatz number plate. With the end of Old Oak Common steam, the Castles became redundant and only two days later, on 9th September, No. 7036 was withdrawn. It made a further journey for store at Oxford before going to Cashmore's Great Bridge in June 1964. The Clevedon branch (from the bay on the left of the photograph) lingered on until 3rd October 1966. (Hugh Ballantyne)

**Left:** Laira based No. 6023 *King Edward II* in immaculate blue livery near Starcross with the down 'Cornish Riviera Express' on 20th February 1951. One of the later-built Kings (6/30), No. 6023 was withdrawn from Cardiff Canton shed in September 1962. It was one of the two engines of the class fortunate enough to go to Woodham Bros scrapyard, Barry, whence it was rescued; it is presently a project for long term restoration at the Great Western Society's depot at Didcot. Again the train is mostly Hawksworth post-war stock; a restaurant-car pair comprising a third class saloon and a kitchen/first class dining saloon completes the rake. The milepost reads 200¾ (from Paddington via Bristol – a route NOT taken by this train). (P. M. Alexander/Millbrook House Collection)

**Right:** With the classic Parson's Rock in the background No. 6025 *King Henry III* takes the first portion of a Kingswear, Paignton, Torquay-Paddington express through Dawlish sometime in the mid-1950s when it was a Laira engine. Note the typical GWR 'spear' fencing and the considerable space in the car park – it was still the age of the train. No. 6025 was built in July 1930, ending its days at Old Oak Common in December 1962, one of the last of its class to be withdrawn. Along with Nos. 6012 and 6029, it was kept to work Newbury Race trains until the eleventh hour. (Millbrook House Collection)

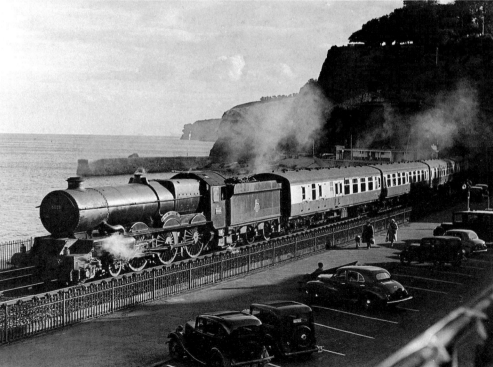

**Right:** Newton Abbot station with the up 9.05 am Paignton to Sheffield (Mon/Fri only) and 'Mayflower', side-by-side on 16th August 1957. This was the beginning of the period for the reintroduction of chocolate and cream coaches on the Western Region; 'The Mayflower', 8.30 am from Plymouth to Paddington, was named in the summer of that year and almost certainly used stock in this livery. The Sheffield train, with LMS design stock, still carries the initial BR livery and has not yet changed to BR maroon. The leading vehicle is one of an interesting series of integral 'all-steel' brake thirds dating from 1930-31. 'The Mayflower' was due out at 9.26 am and the Sheffield at 9.33 am. 'The Mayflower' is headed by No. 6025 *King Henry III* of Plymouth Laira (83D) and the Sheffield by No. 4096 *Highclere Castle* (6/26-1/63) of Bristol Bath Road (82A). (John Robertson/Colour Rail)

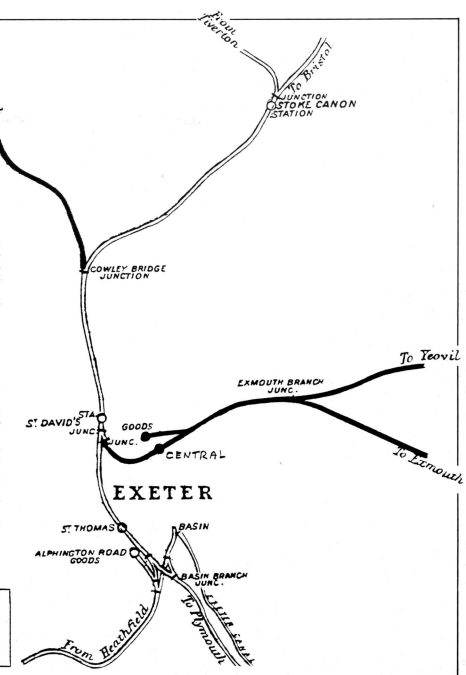

NEWTON S.ᵗ CYRES

From Plymouth

From Tiverton

To Bristol

JUNCTION
STOKE CANON
STATION

COWLEY BRIDGE
JUNCTION

To Yeovil

EXMOUTH BRANCH
JUNC.

S.ᵗ DAVID'S
JUNC.

STA.
JUNC.

GOODS

CENTRAL

To Exmouth

EXETER

S.ᵗ THOMAS

BASIN

ALPHINGTON ROAD
GOODS

BASIN BRANCH
JUNC.

From Heathfield

To Plymouth

**EXPLANATION**

WESTERN REGION

SOUTHERN REGION

**Opposite, below:** Train No. 212 was the 9.10 am service from Manchester London Road to Paignton and is seen leaving Exeter St. Davids at 4.39 pm on 5th August 1955. The Western Region worked it from Bristol onwards; the sheds concerned were usually Bristol Bath Road (82A) and Newton Abbot (83A). On this occasion No. 5024 *Carew Castle* (4/34-5/62) is returning to its home depot. It was one of the early members of the class to be withdrawn. The coaches are in the first BR livery of 'blood and custard' and are all of LMS design, though the second vehicle (a composite with circular 'porthole' toilet windows) was one of several 'LMS' types not actually built until early BR days.

The centre island platform at St. Davids was used mainly for Southern trains to and from Exeter Central and North Devon and North Cornwall stations. The loco shed was to the left of the main up platform. The bracket signal has two 'backing' arms for trains reversing out of Platform 5. Note the bell fixed to the signal post to warn staff using the barrow crossing of approaching trains. (John Robertson Collection/Colour-Rail)

**Right:** Newton Abbot shed on 18th May 1958 with Old Oak Common (81A) based No. 4089 *Donnington Castle* (7/25-10/64) coaled up and ready to go. Newton Abbot was the shed for the Torquay and Kingswear line as well as for the Dainton bankers and often the West to North expresses to Shrewsbury – a long turn for the crew. On shed are Nos. 1023 *County of Oxford*, 5195 and 7000 *Viscount Portal* (behind No. 4089 *Donnington Castle*), 6988 *Swithland Hall*, 5108, 5154 and 4145. An old GWR auto trailer is used as temporary office accommodation – a new building was put up the following year. (Hugh Ballantyne)

**Left:** Newly fitted with a double chimney (3/56) No. 6010 *King Charles II* allocated to Laira (83D) and Britannia Pacific No. 70019 *Lightning* (still with a hand rail on the smoke deflector) make haste through Aller Junction ready for the steep climb up Dainton on 7th July 1956. The train is the down 'Cornish Riviera Express' which must have been heavily loaded. The restaurant car appears to be an old GWR vehicle. The Britannia would have been the pilot engine – coupled behind the train engine in accordance with normal GWR practice. Its tender is piled high with coal whilst that on the King appears to be quite low. No. 6010 was one of the 1928 batch of Kings (April) and lasted until June 1962 when it was withdrawn from Cardiff Canton (88A), though it was stored at Old Oak Common until November 1963. *Lighting* was at that time a Laira (83D) engine, moving to Cardiff Canton at the end of the year. (C. F. H. Oldham)

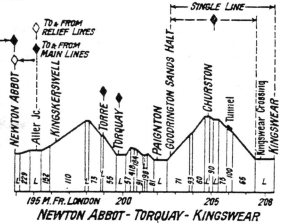

**NEWTON ABBOT - TORQUAY - KINGSWEAR**

**Left:** Another photograph of No. 5082 *Swordfish* (81A) as it climbs high above the cliffs and coves of Torbay with the down 'Torbay Express'. Warships lie at anchor off Torquay in the far distance. It is 21st May 1956 and the train is up to date being made up of an eight coach formation of Mk 1 stock. The single line (now a section of Dart Valley Railway) begins at Goodrington – the only such section on the old GWR which could take double red route engines – the climb is a steady 1:71 and 1:60 to Churston. (P. F. Bowles)

**Right:** It is 11.25 am at Kingswear, terminus of the single line from Paignton, and the up 'Torbay Express' (reporting number 520) is leaving behind No. 5053 *Earl Cairns* on 18th September 1957. To the right, on the other side of the water, is Dartmouth station – a rarity as it had no platforms and never saw a train, only a GWR/WR ferry. Kingswear is now a terminus for the Dart Valley Railway, but the loco yard, carriage sidings and goods yard have all gone, as has the turntable (the GWR also had one at Goodrington for terminating Paignton trains). In the foreground carrying a stopping train head-lamp is No. 7029 *Clun Castle* with a Hawksworth straight sided tender and still retaining its single chimney (double chimney 10/59). No. 5053 was built in May 1936 as *Bishop's Castle* changing its name (taken from the Earl class 32XX 4-4-0) in August 1937. It was withdrawn in July 1962. No. 7029 was more fortunate, it stayed in service to the end of GWR/WR steam and is now at the Birmingham Railway Museum, Tyseley. Both engines were allocated to Newton Abbot. (D. S. Fish)

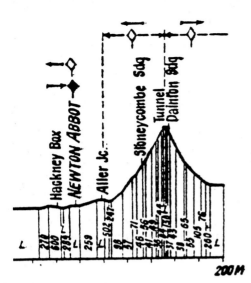

**Above:** No. 7027 *Thornbury Castle* (8/49), an Old Oak Common engine (81A), brings 'The Royal Duchy', 1.30 pm ex-Paddington to Penzance up towards Dainton summit on 17th May 1958. Introduced in 1957, most of the train is made up of BR Mk I chocolate and cream painted stock though the first coach (a strengthening vehicle) is ex-GWR, still painted 'blood and custard'. Mr. Stanley Raymond had yet to make his appearance as GM at Paddington with instructions (and a will) to 'break up the GWR'. No. 7027 ended her active BR life in December 1963 and was lucky enough to go to Woodham Bros. scrapyard at Barry whence it was rescued in August 1972. It is now undergoing restoration jointly by the Birmingham Railway Museum and Dumbleton Hall Limited. (Hugh Ballantyne)

**Left:** Another view of No. 7029 *Clun Castle,* a Newton Abbot (83A) engine at the time. The scene is near Stoneycombe siding where the gradient is 1:46. It is the summer of 1953 and the all red and cream train is the down 'Cornishman' (named in June 1952) from Wolverhampton to Penzance via Stratford upon Avon, Cheltenham and Gloucester. The train contains a reburbished GWR composite dining car and carries 'Cornishman' boards under the cantrail of the BR Mk I coaches. At that time there was no locomotive headboard. (H. J. Ashman)

**Above:** Twisting round the Cornish curves No. 4095 *Harlech Castle* (6/26-12/62), a Penzance (83G) based engine – one of their two Castles, the other being No. 5020 *Trematon Castle* – takes the 6.20 pm Penzance to Kensington milk train into Chacewater station on 16th May 1959. Chacewater was the junction station for the line which went off to Newquay and looped back to Par. (M. Mensing)

**Right:** Two Laira based Kings on their home shed on 26th March 1950, a scene which would have been ideal in colour as No. 6025 *King Henry III* (7/30-6/62) was in experimental blue lined out in red whilst No. 6012 *King Edward VI* (4/28-12/62) was still in GWR dark green. Note the differing inside valve and spindle covers. The WR was very quick to remove the G (crest) W from its tenders and substituting British Railways but in Great Western style letters. (P. M. Alexander/Millbrook House Collection)

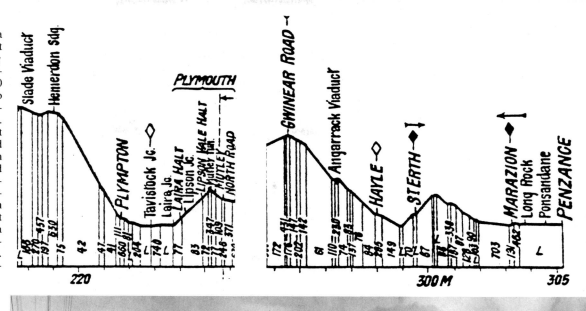

**Opposite:** In what is almost a GWR scene, one of the first Kings (7/27) No. 6001 *King Edward VII* climbs Hemerdon bank, 1:42, with the 2.00 pm express from Plymouth to Paddington (11.00 am ex-Penzance) on 3rd June 1954. The stock is all Great Western. No. 6001 finished up as a Wolverhampton Stafford Road engine and was withdrawn on the dieselisation of the London-Birmingham services in September 1962. The first vehicle appears to be a strengthener, a ten compartment GWR toplight third. (M. W. Earley Collection-NRM)

**Right:** With a Hawksworth brake third at the head of the train, No. 5021 *Whittington Castle* (8/32-9/62) climbs the 1:67, out of St. Erth on 16th June 1950. The train is likely to be a down express and No. 5021 is shedded at Plymouth, Laira (83D). It has no shed plate and the allocation was still marked on the front frame adjacent to the buffer beam as in GWR practice, though scarcely visible; the lettering is LA. (C. F. H. Oldham)

# THE SOUTH WALES MAIN LINE

**Right:** A rare shot of a King on one of the South Wales runs at Pilning. No. 6019 *King Henry V* of Cardiff Canton (now 88A) at the head of train 1A58 the 8.00 Neyland-Paddington breasting the summit and entering the station in 1962. Once again there is a Great Western restaurant car in the train's otherwise BR Mk I makeup. It is the third vehicle along; note the different and more substantial vehicle profile – indication of the generous GWR loading gauge. The first ever allocation of Kings to Cardiff took effect during the winter timetable for 1960, many engines being transferred in August due to the dieselisation of the West of England main line. (Hugh Ballantyne)

**Below:** With a later (38XX) Great Western 2-8-0 in the background, No. 4094 *Dynevor Castle* (5/26-3/62) allocated to Canton (86C) heads a local train into Carmarthen station in September 1950. The shed was adjacent to the up platform and easy to photograph. The train is probably from Paddington to Pembroke Dock or Milford Haven, stopping at most stations. (P. M. Alexander/Millbrook House Collection)

**Left:** Cardiff Canton (86C) based No. 7022 *Hereford Castle* (6/49-6/65) – later to become one of the last active Castles at Gloucester Horton Road (85B) – climbs the 1:100 out of the Severn Tunnel with the 10.35 am (SuO) Cardiff to Paddington at Pilning on 10th September 1950. With the coming of the BR Britannia 4-6-2s in late 1956 (Canton was the only WR depot to accept them), the Castles there drifted away over the next eighteen months, later to be partially replaced by Kings. (P. M. Alexander/Millbrook House Collection)

**Below:** A late 1950s photograph of No. 5016 *Montgomery Castle* (7/32-9/62), then based at Swansea Landore shed (87E), shows the locomotive emerging from Newport West tunnel towards the station with the 9.53 am Pembroke Dock to Paddington express. Note ringed bracket signal arms for the goods line and the Great Western shunters' truck behind the 57XX class 0-6-0 pannier tank. (G. F. Heiron)

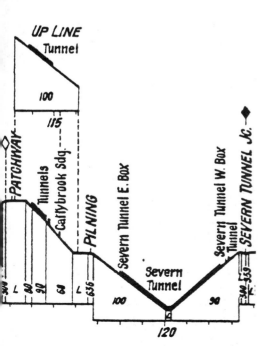

**Above:** The up Pembroke Coast Express approaching Newport (Monmouthshire) on the four track section between St Brides signal box and Ebbw Junction. The train left Pembroke Dock at 1.05 pm and called at principal stations to Swansea then Cardiff, Newport and Paddington. The locomotive is Castle class No. 4095 *Harlech Castle* built at Swindon in June 1926 and withdrawn in December 1962. The coaches are all BR Mk I corridors except for the Restaurant Car which may be a refurbished GW composite originally built in 1922. The Castle and the first four vehicles were attached at Swansea High Street where the train reversed and the rear four, brake to brake, came through from Pembroke Dock. (R. J. Blenkinsop)

**Below:** The up Pembroke Coast Express approaches Gaer Junction Newport (Monmouthshire) west of the station hauled by a Castle. The formation appears to be the same as the train shown above. The track layout here was very complicated. The train is on the main line which crosses from the north pair of tracks to the south and continues through the original South Wales Railway tunnel. The Western Valleys lines trail in from the left and continue as the relief lines through the 'new' tunnel opened in 1912. There is also a connection from relief to main beyond the signal box which prior to September 1950 was a 'scissors' crossing also with a connection from relief to main. (G. F. Heiron)

**Right:** Castle class No. 5080 *Defiant* at Cardiff Canton shed in the mid 50s. 5080 was built at Swindon in May 1939 and was originally named *Ogmore Castle*. Nos. 5071 to 5082 were renamed after R.A.F aircraft between September 1940 and January 1941. *"Defiant"* was withdrawn in April 1963 but was preserved and rebuilt at the Tyseley locomotive works of the Birmingham Railway Museum. Despite the prevailing post-war austerity Canton depot always kept its main line locomotives in pristine condition as seen here. (R. C. Riley)

**Below:** Star class 4-6-0 No. 4023 heads a football excursion on 9th October 1948 from either Swansea or Llanelly to Paddington (the headboard reads *Llanelly Rover*), at Severn Tunnel Junction. 4023 was built at Swindon in June 1909 and named *King George*. When the 1927 series of Kings were built it was renamed *Danish Monarch*. This second name was removed in November 1940 not doubt because Denmark was then under German occupation. Withdrawal came in July 1952. The train is on the 'Up Tunnel' line with the signal off for the train to proceed through the tunnel (the longest on BR), to Paddington. (P. M. Alexander)

# PADDINGTON TO CHESTER VIA BIRMINGHAM

**Below:** Once the new Castles were allocated to Oxford shed (Nos. 7008 *Swansea Castle* and 7010 *Avondale Castle* arrived during 1949), the depot's Stars began to be passed over to secondary workings and freights. This was apparently the fate of No. 4049 *Princess Maud* (5/14-7/53) until transfer to Wolverhampton Stafford Road (84A) in August 1950. Members of the class would have worked a number of secondary expresses but also the through Margate-Birkenhead trains usually as far as Wolverhampton; though some ran right through to Shrewsbury which also had an allocation of Stars. Filling in time and nearly nine months before transfer, No. 4049 heads a down express freight (partially fitted) at West Ruislip. The new London Transport Central Line extension had just been opened and is to the right of the picture. (C. R. L. Coles)

**Right:** One of the 1914 built Stars, No. 4060 *Princess Eugenie*, takes the nine coach 4.20 pm Wolverhampton to Paddington express through Princes Risborough on Saturday 2nd September 1950; it is a motley collection of ex Great Western stock. At the time, No. 4060 was a Wolverhampton Stafford Road (84A) engine though two months later it was transferred to Bristol Bath Road (82A) whence it was withdrawn in October 1952 with the influx of BR built Castles and Britannias. The GWR and GC Joint line ran from Northolt Junction to Ashendon Junction and allowed both companies an improved service to London from the north without competing with each other. (J. F. Russell-Smith Collection-NRM)

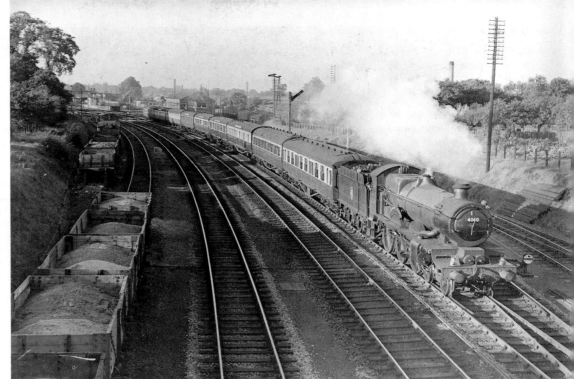

**Left:** Banbury North Junction in October 1948 with No. 5018 *St. Mawes Castle* (7/32-3/64) double heading an unknown Grange class 4-6-0 on a Sunday Paddington to Birkenhead express. No. 5018 was then a Stafford Road (84A) engine and the train (with coach roof boards) was a late afternoon one. Note the 70ft 'Concertina' leading coach with recessed doors (already over 40 years old) now being used as a Sunday strengthener. The photograph was taken from Banbury North Junction Box which controlled the entrance of the ex-GC, later LNER line from Woodford. The pilot engine, coupled behind the Castle in good GWR practice, may well have come on at Banbury for the climb up to Harbury and Hatton – the 'Concertina' being one over the load for a Castle on this road. (P. B. Whitehouse)

33

**Right:** The pioneer King, No. 6000 *King George V* (built at Swindon in June 1927 and now preserved in the National Collection), emerges from the short Harbury tunnel with the up 'Cambrian Coast Express' in May 1960 just before the introduction of four figure reporting numbers. The leading coaches are in chocolate and cream – a livery re-introduced when the Regions were given greater autonomy in the mid 1950s but soon to be obliterated by BR's policy of removing things which appeared to be linked with the Great Western. (T. E. Williams Collection-NRM)

**Below:** Double chimney No. 5064 *Bishop's Castle* (6/37-9/62), then allocated to Gloucester Horton Road depot and nearing the end of its life, approaches the summit of Hatton bank on the 1:100 climb from just north of Warwick on a summer Saturday in 1962. This was the last summer of steam on the Paddington to Wolverhampton services, the diesels taking over in the autumn, displacing the Kings and leaving only a few Castles in reserve for reliefs. The train is in the all-maroon livery adopted by BR for all regions (except the SR) in 1956 but not 100% universal on the Western Region until after the final abandonment of chocolate and cream – see previous view. (P. B. Whitehouse)

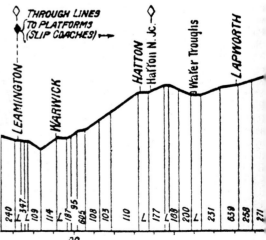

**Left:** A very dirty No. 5014 *Goodrich Castle* (6/32-2/65) of Old Oak Common shed (81A) approaches Knowle and Dorridge station on 26th August 1951 with an up express. It is on the main line; the tracks on the left are the relief lines put in during the 1933 Olton to Lapworth widening and removed from 2nd January 1968. The leading coach is one of the 1905 'Dreadnoughts' with recessed doors, its toplights covered over with steel panels. The roof ventilators show how the corridor changed sides in the middle of the vehicle. The 'Dreadnoughts' were the largest carriages in Britain when first built and nearly all were withdrawn in this early BR period. They were early examples of GWR carriages built without individual external compartment doors but this idea was never wholly accepted on the old GWR and such compartments did not return again until the 1930s and even then were not universal. (C. F. H. Oldham)

**Right:** A scene eleven years on (11th May 1963), this time at the south end of Knowle and Dorridge station with a train on the up relief line; it could well be the 8.42 am Salop to Paddington parcels train which dawdled about and was due here around 3.20 pm; this was booked over the relief line. By now all the Castles and Kings had gone from the Birmingham express services and only had odd jobs to do. No. 7024 *Powis Castle* (6/49-2/65) was then an Oxley engine as the shed at Stafford Road was due to close the following September with the regional transfer of routes north of Banbury and Craven Arms to the LMR. The closure of Snow Hill station was soon to follow – in March 1967 to all but a few local services and final extinction on 6th March 1972. (C. F. H. Oldham)

**Right:** No. 4094 *Dynevor Castle* (Landore shed 87E) shunts the empty coaching stock for a Barry Island excursion out of Tyseley carriage sidings whence it will cross over into Platform 4 – to the right of the picture. It is Whit Sunday, 5th June 1960, and the train will run via Stourbridge Junction and Worcester – off the regular beat for a Castle. As most trains originating at Birmingham had to be worked from Tyseley as empty stock, excursions leaving Snow Hill in the down direction were quite often scheduled to pick up passengers from the suburban stations at Tyseley, Small Heath and Bordesley en route into Birmingham. (M. Mensing)

**Below:** Moor Street station Birmingham (closed 26th September 1987) with No. 5065 *Newport Castle* (1/37-1/63) then allocated to Old Oak Common shed (81A) arriving on the 1.11 pm from Portsmouth Harbour. It is heading a train of Southern stock – mostly Maunsell but with what looks like a Bullied coach fourth from the engine. No. 036 (properly 1036) the reporting number on the engine is not one from the Southern Region but originated from the LMR and it may be assumed that this failed to be removed at Oxford on a down journey. The date is 2nd July 1960; Moor Street station was used for certain holiday trains like this in the summer, to relieve pressure on Snow Hill. These holiday trains required compulsory seat reservation. (M. Mensing)

EXCURSION

— TO —

# NEWPORT, CARDIFF
(MON.) (GENERAL)

AND

# BARRY ISLAND

WHIT SUNDAY, 5th JUNE

| FROM TRAIN No. X59 | Depart | RETURN FARES—SECOND CLASS | | | DUE BACK |
| | | Newport | Cardiff | Barry Island | |
|---|---|---|---|---|---|
| | a.m. | s. d. | s. d. | s. d. | night |
| Tyseley | 9 25 | | | | 12 20 |
| Small Heath and Sparkbrook | 9 30 | | | | 12 15 |
| Bordesley | 9 34 | | | | 12 10 |
| BIRMINGHAM (Snow Hill) | 9 40 | | | | 12 5 |
| Smethwick West | 9 50 | | | | 11 55 |
| Oldbury and Langley Green | 9 55 | | | | 11 50 |
| Rowley Regis and Blackheath | 10 0 | 14/6 | 16/- | 17/6 | 11 45 |
| Old Hill | 10 5 | | | | 11 40 |
| Cradley Heath and Cradley | 10 5 | | | | 11 35 |
| Lye | 10 15 | | | | 11 30 |
| Stourbridge Junction | 10 25 | | | | 11 15 |
| ARRIVAL TIMES | | p.m. 1 10 | p.m. 1 30 | p.m. 2 0 | |
| RETURN TIMES—SAME DAY | | p.m. 8 30 | p.m. 8 10 | p.m. 7 40 | |

H.D.

## PARKING OF CARS AND MOTOR CYCLES

If you use your car or motor cycle for your journeys between your home and the station, you will find the station parking facilities of great convenience. These facilities are provided at a number of stations at reasonable fees and season tickets are available for regular patrons. Full particulars may be obtained from British Railways stations.

**Above:** One of the last three Stars to remain in service No. 4056 *Princess Margaret* (7/14-10/57) stands very smartly groomed in Tyseley passenger roundhouse on 8th September 1956 prior to hauling a Stephenson Locomotive Society special to Swindon works the following day. The engine, Laira (83D), has been cleaned and its BR shed and front number plates temporarily removed, both being replaced by the number painted on the buffer beam and TYS on the running plate behind the buffer beam in true Great Western fashion. It is a typical Saturday afternoon shed scene generally quiet and, in this case, clean – thus giving the lie to the tale that all sheds were filthy in BR days. (P. B. Whitehouse)

**Right:** Snow Hill station Birmingham on the morning of 25th July 1956 with Star class 4-6-0 No. 4061 *Glastonbury Abbey* (5/22-3/57) during the last years of its life. It is at the head of the first 'express' of the day to Birkenhead, originating at Leamington Spa at 7.45 am and doubling as a semi fast commuter train to Birmingham. It usually conveyed some non corridor stock – eg the leading vehicle. At that time the engine was allocated to Wolverhampton Stafford Road (84A) whence it was withdrawn – before then it had been at Shrewsbury (84G). One of the delights of Snow Hill was its abundance of poster boards still extant and flourishing in the mid-1950s; immediately to the right of the smokebox there is that excellent poster showing a BR Standard Class 4 4-6-0 on the Cambrian, whilst next to it is a typical Western view of Glorious Devon. (M. Mensing)

**Below:** A Sunday scene at Snow Hill with track repairs in progress on the up roads on 9th October 1960. By now the platforms had been signalled for bi-directional running (11.9.60) and No. 6006 *King George I* (2/28-2/62), a Stafford Road (84A) engine, draws into No. 5 (normally the down main line platform) with a Wolverhampton to Paddington express. The remains of Snow Hill South Box can just be seen under the bridge to the right. With the advent of colour light resignalling, the new power box was situated in the platform building behind the old bookstall. (P. H. Wells)

**Right:** The up 'Inter-City' (4.35 pm from Wolverhampton and 5.00 pm from Birmingham Snow Hill) passes West Bromwich behind No. 6000 *King George V*, an Old Oak Common engine, on 29th September 1958. The stock is Mk I and a hundred per cent chocolate and cream. In four years' time this would all be changed. (M. Mensing)

**Below:** The dreadful Stafford Road shed in the early morning of Saturday 24th August 1963. The Kings have departed to their last rest and the shed itself is about to close leaving Oxley as the Wolverhampton depot. The occupants at the time this photograph was taken were mostly local residents No. 7001 *Sir James Milne* (5/46) and named *Denbigh Castle* until 2/48 (withdrawn in 9/63 from Worcester after running the last WR express steam passenger trains), No. 5026 *Criccieth Castle* (4/34-11/64) later an Oxley (2B) engine, and No. 7006 *Lydford Castle* (6/46-12/63) of Old Oak Common (81A). They are being prepared for Saturday Only trains from Wolverhampton Low Level; these services would be the 8.10 am to Weston-super-Mare, the 8.43 am to Portsmouth Harbour and the 10.05 am to Kingswear. (Hugh Ballantyne)

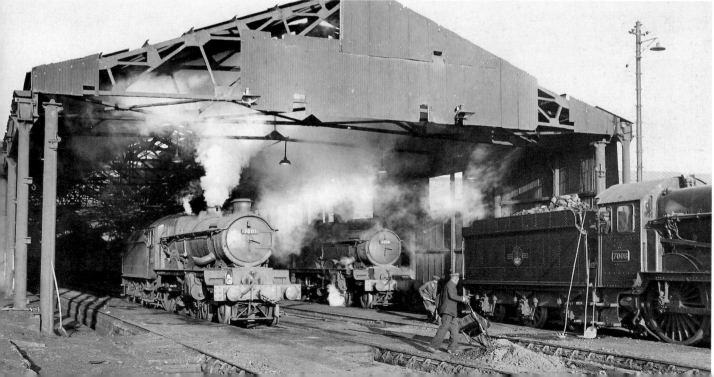

**Right:** Shrewsbury on 14th May 1949 with Oxford based (OXF) Star No. 4049 *Princess Maud* (5/14-7/53) on the Birkenhead to Margate through train, probably composed of Southern stock. This was a normal Oxford working as engines were changed there. An LMS Black Five 4-6-0 No. 44837 waits on the right with a Crewe to Hereford freight. Although Shrewsbury was a joint station, the LNWR (later LMS) was responsible for all signalling and its characteristic semaphores can be seen on the right of the picture. (P. M. Alexander/Millbrook House Collection)

**Below:** Indian Summer at Shrewsbury. The up 'Cambrian Coast Express' awaits the right away on a summer's day in 1962. The engine is No. 7025 *Sudeley Castle* (8/49-9/64) (another example later to be allocated to Worcester for the London expresses) of Shrewsbury shed (89A). (P. B. Whitehouse)

**Above:** A scene near Saltney Junction in July 1950 with No. 5075 *Wellington* (8/38 – until 10/40 *Devizes Castle* – withdrawn 9/62 from Bristol St. Phillips Marsh) on the 12.25 pm Birkenhead to Pwllheli, 1.20 from Chester. The Castle will have come off at Ruabon where the train went forward with either a Manor class 4-6-0 or a 43XX class Mogul. The engine is Chester (84K) based and carries the full British Railways' lettering in Great Western style on its tender. (Eric Treacy/Millbrook House Collection)

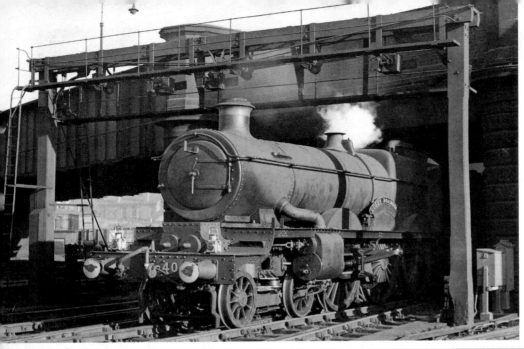

**Left:** Another Shrewsbury (89A) engine: Star class No. 4040 *Queen Boadicea* (3/11-6/51) at Chester with a Birkenhead to Paddington express probably in July 1950. These trains usually had three classes of engine for their journey – a 43XX Mogul, a 51XX 2-6-2 tank or even an LMS engine, from Birkenhead to Chester, a Star or Castle to Wolverhampton (Low Level) and a King or a Castle to Paddington. (Eric Treacy/Millbrook House Collection)

**Below:** A Castle at Chester. No. 5033 *Broughton Castle* (5/35-9/62) – an Old Oak Common (81A) engine for many years – stands alongside the magnificent No. 4 LNWR signalbox and is surrounded by a semi-'forest' of LNWR semaphore signals, whilst waiting to back down on a train for Wolverhampton. In the background is Chester GWR shed with a couple of 2-6-2 tanks alongside and a further unknown Castle behind. On the right is an LMS Stanier Black Five 4-6-0. The date is probably July 1950. (Eric Treacy/Millbrook House Collection)

# HEREFORD – WORCESTER – OXFORD

**Right:** Sheer lift. Worcester works had no means of either dropping the wheels out of a locomotive or lifting it wholesale depending, as did other minor works, on the old GWR system of using a pair of sheer legs. No. 5094 *Tretower Castle* (6/39-9/62) receives one of its last heavy casual repairs at Worcester 'Factory' on 21st October 1961. The Works Manager, Don Green, to the right of the picture, supervises the operation. No. 5094 was then a Bristol St. Phillips Marsh (82B) engine, Bath Road having closed to become a diesel depot in 1960. (Millbrook House Collection)

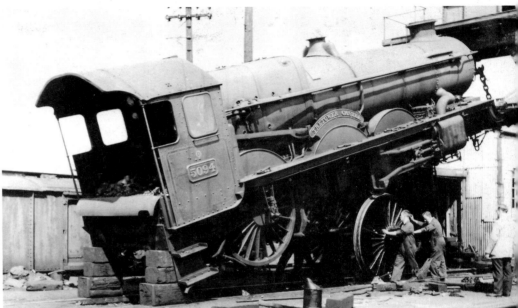

**Left:** The 11.50 am from Hereford to Paddington leaves Worcester Shrub Hill and passes Wylds Lane yard on 25th July 1961. The engine is Worcester based (85A) No. 7007 *Great Western* (7/46-2/63) the last GWR-built Castle and named to commemorate the Great Western Railway. On the right is No. 4945 *Milligan Hall* a Southall (81C) engine with a Stourbridge Junction to Stoke Gifford freight. (Millbrook House Collection)

**Left:** Rebuilt from an original Star, Castle class No. 5092 *Tresco Abbey* (4/38-7/63) of Worcester shed (85A) takes an up Oxford and Paddington express over the summit of Campden bank south of Honeybourne on 11th October 1952. This was very much a racing ground for down trains. When the engines for the last Paddington to Plymouth 'all steam' run on 9th May 1964 were being selected, it was not unknown to reach 100 mph on this section, albeit momentarily. (T. E. Williams Collection-NRM)

**Below:** On 7th September 1949 and within a month of withdrawal Star No. 4019 *Knight Templar* (5/08-10/49) enters Charlbury near Kingham (the junction for Cheltenham and Banbury) with an up OWW (Oxford, Worcester and Wolverhampton) local. No. 4019 was rather off its normal route as it was a Bristol Bath Road (82A) engine. A point worth noting for modellers is the soot encrusted arch of the over-bridge – far darker and dirtier on the side attacked by engines departing from the platform. (P. H. Wells)

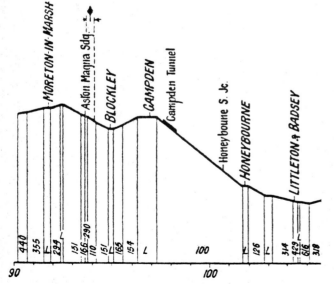

**Right:** Oxford station on 24th August 1952 with No. 5086 *Viscount Horne* (12/37-12/58) waiting for the right away with an up express. There is a nice selection of Great Western signals complete with route indicators. Note the disc (red) with the GWR power classification D carried to the end of steam – a piece of GWR never to disappear. (T. E. Williams Collection-NRM)

**Opposite:** Cardiff General station (extensively rebuilt in the early 1930s) with No. 5061 *Earl of Birkenhead* from Canton shed (88A) at the head of 1M72 (11.50 am Swansea-Manchester) West to North express for Shrewsbury c 1961. No. 5061 (6/37) was originally named *Sudeley Castle* (a name later carried by No. 7025) until October 1937 when it took one of the names originally given to the 32XX Duke/Bulldog rebuilds. The Canton cleaners were either lazy or in short supply – the shed's engines were usually exemplarily turned out – as only the cab sides and splashers have received attention. The shed closed for conversion to a diesel depot in September 1962 when most of its Castle allocation, including No. 5061 went for scrap. (G. F. Heiron)

**Right:** Less than a year old and dirty to boot, No. 7028 *Cadbury Castle* (5/50-12/63) of Landore shed (87E) climbs the 1:82 section of the seven mile bank between Penpergwm and Llanvihangel with a Sunday Cardiff to Manchester train, made up of ex-LMS and Great Western stock, on 25th March 1951. (P. M. Alexander/Millbrook House Collection)

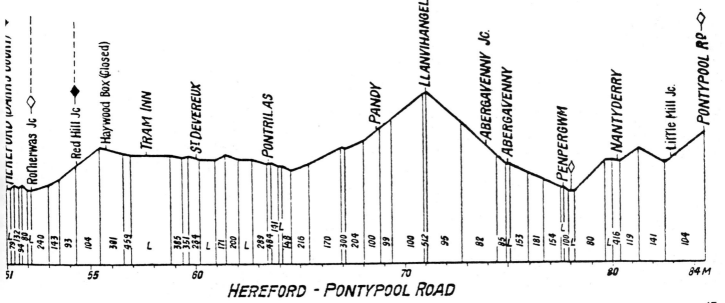

HEREFORD - PONTYPOOL ROAD

**Above:** Only just into Nationalisation, 6th November 1948, Star No. 4039 *Queen Matilda* (2/11-11/50) still without outside steam pipes is being prepared for a Cardiff train on Hereford shed. It is a Landore (LDR) engine and remained so until withdrawal. (P. M. Alexander/Millbrook House Collection)

**Above:** Hereford station in the late summer of 1948 with No. 5020 *Trematon Castle* (7/32-11/62) on a south bound train composed of ex Great Western and LMS stock, probably the 9.25 am Liverpool-Penzance (1.05 pm from Hereford). The engine has been repainted in the last Great Western livery with the company crest in between the letters G and W; it was then allocated to Cardiff Canton (CDF). The carriages are a delightful mixture. Leading is a GWR 'Sunshine' corridor coach of the late 1930s, followed by a bow-ended corridor with outside doors to all compartments. The first LMS vehicle is of LNWR origin, the second is a wood panelled standard vehicle of the 1920s and is followed by Stanier stock. (P. B. Whitehouse)

**Right:** Shrewsbury station in September 1960 with No. 5072 *Hurricane* (6/38 and *Compton Castle* until 1/40; withdrawn 10/62) of Stafford Road shed (84A) on a train from Wolverhampton and the south. On the right No. 5059 *Earl St. Aldwyn* (5/37-6/12) and a Shrewsbury (89A) engine, heads M91 (actually 1M91), the 6.00 am (SO) Penzance to Liverpool. The Western engines will come off here to be replaced by possibly a Britannia 4-6-2 or Black Five 4-6-0 for the trains onward journeys. (P. B. Whitehouse)

# BRISTOL TO BIRMINGHAM

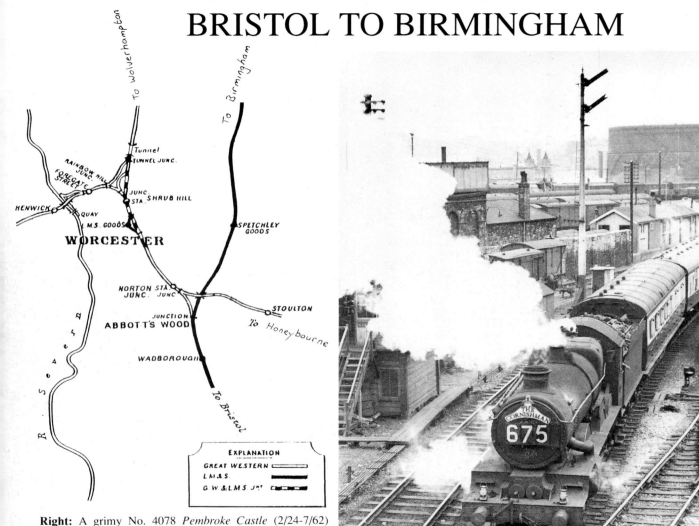

To Wolverhampton

To Birmingham

RAINBOW JUNC.
Tunnel
TUNNEL JUNC.
FOREGATE STREET
JUNC. STA. SHRUB HILL
HENWICK
QUAY
M.S. GOODS
**WORCESTER**
SPETCHLEY GOODS

NORTON STA. JUNC. JUNC.
JUNCTION
**ABBOTT'S WOOD**
STOULTON
To Honeybourne

WADBOROUGH

R. Severn

To Bristol

**EXPLANATION**

| | |
|---|---|
| GREAT WESTERN | ▭▭▭ |
| L.M.&S. | ▬▬▬ |
| G.W.&L.M.S. JNT. | ▭▬▭▬ |

**Right:** A grimy No. 4078 *Pembroke Castle* (2/24-7/62) eases the northbound 'Cornishman' round the curve to engine shed sidings, Bristol, where the waiting banker (right) will assist it up the steep 1:69-90 to Fishponds. The train is using the old MR route (now closed) via Mangotsfield not the GWR via Filton and Stoke Gifford. The date is sometime between November 1958 and July 1959 when No. 4078 was a Bath Road (82A) engine. (G. F. Heiron)

**Above:** A busy moment for the signalman at Norton Junction, Worcester on 23rd April 1957. There has been engineering work on the line between Honeybourne and Cheltenham causing the 9.00 am Wolverhampton to Penzance ('The Cornishman') to be diverted via Evesham and Pershore. No. 7026 *Tenby Castle* (8/49-10/64) is pulling forward towards Worcester where No. 6947 *Helmingham Hall* waits to work the train forward via the Midland line – an interesting piece of railway operation for the enthusiast though not so for the general run of passengers. A down freight behind Churchward 2-8-0 No. 2870 has been shunted on to the up road. (T. E. Williams Collection-NRM)

**Below:** A 1914 Star in the evening of its days: No. 4051 *Princess Helena* (6/14-10/50) takes a Birmingham (Snow Hill) to Worcester semi fast out of Stratford upon Avon on 10th April 1050. No. 4051 was a Worcester engine at the time but carries no shed plate or Great Western type coding. The tender is so dirty that any lettering has been obliterated by grime and the engine is no better – not an advertisement for Worcester cleaners. The train appears to be one of the old Birmingham Division 4-coach wooden bodied compartment suburban sets with snap handles on the outside only. If you could not get the window open to get at the handle and with station stops very short, there were sometimes problems ahead! The screw reverser on these Stars stood right back into the cab and the driver had to be almost on the tender to operate it. The train in the island platform beyond the bridge would be the auto service for Leamington Spa. (C. F. H. Oldham)

**Below:** A crisp view at Stratford upon Avon station on 30th May 1958 with No. 5059 *Earl St. Aldwyn* (5/37 originally *Powis Castle* until 10/37-6/62) on the up 'Cornishman', the 10.40 am Penzance-Wolverhampton, waiting for the right away. No. 5059 has a full head of steam ready for the climb up the 1:75 to Wilmcote; it is obviously not short of water as the driver has stopped well ahead of the column. In all probability there is a banker on the rear, most likely a 2251 class 0-6-0. Stratford shed had both the bankers and some 51XX 2-6-2 tanks for the local services. Sometimes this was a pilot running through to Snow Hill depending on the weight of the train. (T. E. Williams Collection-NRM)

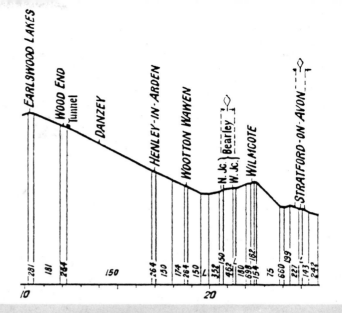

# SWINDON TO GLOUCESTER

**Above:** The battle of the 'Big Hill' is just about over as No. 7023 *Penrice Castle* (6/49-2/65) approaches the portal of Sapperton Tunnel at the head of a London bound express in April 1954. The coaches are a mixed bag of Gresley and Thompson, BR Mk I and LMS stock all in early BR 'Blood and Custard' livery. No. 7023 was allocated to Cardiff Canton (86C) in 1955. (G. F. Heiron)

**Left:** No. 7030 *Cranbrook Castle* (6/50-2/63), an Old Oak Common (81A) engine, approaches St. Mary's Crossing Halt on the way down from Sapperton Tunnel with a Paddington to Cheltenham express during the summer of 1952. A large number of very GWR artefacts abound: the wooden signal post and arms, platelayers' hut, lamp, close-boarded fencing and the cast iron columns for the post and wire fence. (G. F. Heiron)

**Below:** Swindon allocated engine No. 5068 *Beverston Castle* (6/38-9/62), with eight-wheel tender carrying British Railways in GWR lettering, waits at Gloucester on 4th September 1948. This unique 4000 gallon tender (No. 2586) was built in 1931. The extra axle was intended to lessen the load on the bearings, a problem with the ordinary six wheel version. It remained in service until 1963. (P. M. Alexander/Millbrook House Collection)

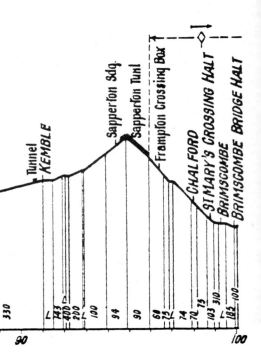

# Wessex Interlude

**Above:** Westbury to Salisbury. Codford station on Saturday 17th September 1955, the last day of passenger services for all the stations between Salisbury and Warminster, officially closed from 19th September. No. 5080 *Defiant*, originally *Ogmore Castle* (5/39 renamed 1/41) double heads No. 4968 *Shotton Hall* on the 5.02 pm Salisbury-Cardiff. It was the last up train to call at Codford (5.30 pm) and nine passengers alighted. No. 5080 was withdrawn in April 1963 from Llanelly shed and was purchased by Woodham Bros., Barry from where it was rescued in August 1974, originally for spares at the Birmingham Railway Museum, Tyseley. Fortunately it was found possible to restore it to full working order and No. 5080 re-entered main line service in 1988. (Hugh Ballantyne)

**Below:** A Weymouth bound express from Paddington at Sparkford on 10th September 1951. The engine is No. 5076 *Gladiator* (8/38-9/64), *Drysllwyn Castle* until renamed 1/41. These services were withdrawn from the summer of 1960, all traffic then being routed out of Waterloo. Only DMUs or Sprinters from Bristol now use this section. Sparkford station closed in October 1966. (T. E. Williams Collection-NRM)

# Trials

**Above:** The 1948 Trials. The Great Western locomotives taking part in the 1948 exchange trials were unable to travel over several of the chosen routes due to clearance problems; the Kings being the most restricted. No. 6018, *King Henry VI* was the engine selected for the trials over the East coast route between King's Cross and Leeds and it is seen here climbing past Beeston Junction with the 7.50 am to King's Cross on 21st May 1948. The Great Western King was one of two 4-6-0s in the express passenger category (the only class 7P) and its trial results were disappointing compared with the essentially more modern types of the other companies. This was partly due to its low degree of superheating and also the hard coal used (the Great Western engines were built for the softer and less smoky Welsh steam coal), although deteriorating quality of coal was to become an ever increasing problem for all regions through the 1950s. (Eric Treacy/Millbrook House Collection)

**Below:** The 1953 Swindon Trial. The poor showing in the 1948 trials prompted Swindon into action and a series of test runs over the GW main line bettered the fuel economy of their products when using soft Welsh coal. However, the search for improvement continued in both superheating and blast pipe arrangements. A series of dynamometer car trials between Reading and Stoke Gifford in July 1953, using No. 6001 *King Edward VII*, were part of this process. On the fourth day of the trials, 2nd July 1953, a 25 coach train of 796 tons was hauled over this route at an average speed of 60 mph. Alterations to No. 6001's blast pipe arrangement proved successful and allowed pre-war schedules on the top express trains to be reintroduced even with poorer quality coal. This view of the tests was taken at Hullavington; a tarpaulin having been provided to make conditions behind the indicating shelter a little more comfortable! The final outcome of the draughting tests, which were not confined to Swindon types, was the fitting of double blast pipes and chimneys to the Kings and many of the Castles. (P. M. Alexander/Millbrook House Collection)

**Left:** 'The Inter-City' headboard fitted to No. 5022 *Wigmore Castle* (8/32-9/62) on the up train standing at Snow Hill station, Birmingham in 1957; the engine was then allocated to Wolverhampton Stafford Road depot (84A). Note the Western Region practice of machining the smoke box number plate figures – other Regions left them as cast. Another Swindon refinement of quality! The headboard was painted in chocolate and cream carrying the coats of arms of London (top), Birmingham (left) and Wolverhampton. (M. Mensing)

# Names,
# Liveries and
# Deceptions

**Right:** The nameplate and centre splasher of Star class No. 4062 *Malmesbury Abbey* (5/22-11/56) on 30th April 1950 at Swindon works. The engine is in BR lined dark green. Note the absence of splasher beading and that the engine is in forward gear. The tyres seem to be thin though there are still six years of life ahead for this engine. (P. M. Alexander/Millbrook House Collection)

**Left:** A centre side view of No. 5011 *Tintagel Castle* (7-27-9/62) at Swindon in 1950. The engine is repainted and fully lined out in BR dark green livery with highly polished safety valve cover and splasher beading. Note that it is in mid gear, the proper and safe position when standing. (P. M. Alexander/Millbrook House Collection)

**Below left:** A second style of Castle nameplate was used where 'Castle' did not appear in the name itself, the class then being acknowledged by the small brass CASTLE CLASS, set immediately below the name. similar plates in all respects were fitted to the 'Earls' and 'Warplanes' of 1937 and 1940/41. No. 7037 was the last Castle ever to be built; it was named *Swindon* by HRH Princess Elizabeth on 15th November 1950 though actually turned out of works in August. The naming was ostensibly to commemorate the Golden Jubilee of the Borough but other GW minds had obviously been at work too. No. 7037 carried the coat of arms of the Borough of Swindon, where it spent much of its life, though withdrawal was from Old Oak Common in March 1963. (P. M. Alexander/Millbrook House Collection)

**Below right:** An unusual plate for a Great Western engine: *The Somerset Light Infantry (Prince Albert's)*. No. 4016 in its Star form was *Knight of the Golden Fleece* built in 1908 and was an early transformation to a Castle (10/25) retaining its original name. On renaming in January 1938 it was also fitted with plaques of the regimental crest – but no indication that it was a Castle. These early rebuilds were the first to go and No. 4016 was withdrawn at Swindon in September 1951 some eighteen months after this photograph was taken at Newton Abbot on 26th March 1950. (P. M. Alexander/Millbrook House Collection)

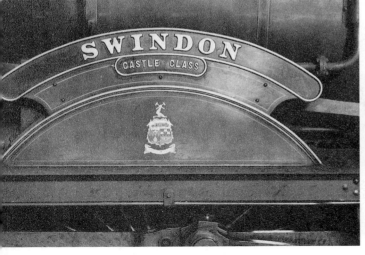

**Above:** No. 7013 *Bristol Castle* (7/48-9/64) masquerading as No. 4082 *Windsor Castle* (the accepted GWR Royal engine) hauling HM King George VI's funeral train on 15th February 1952. No. 4082 (4/24-2/65) was in Swindon works for overhaul at the time of the King's death so a hasty substitution of number and nameplate was made; they were never changed back. The original *Windsor Castle* also carried a commemorative plaque acknowledging that the engine had been driven from Swindon Works to the station by HM King George V; these too were transferred but subsequently removed. The train originated at Wolferton (for Sandringham), prior to the Lying in State in Westminster Hall and comprised the LNER Royal saloons plus supporting vehicles. This photograph shows it on the way from Paddington to Windsor. (M. W. Earley Collection-NRM)

**Below:** Seven months later, on 6th September 1952, No. 7013 (originally No. 4082 *Windsor Castle*) breasts the 1:90 out of Colwall Tunnel with the 5.35 pm Worcester Shrub Hill to Hereford local. (P. M. Alexander/Millbrook House Collection)

# Bibliography

Locomotives of the Great Western Railway *Railway Correspondence and Travel Society,* 1951 onwards.
Railway Clearing House Junction Diagrams, *RCH,* 1928.
Gradients of the Main Line British Railways *The Railway Publishing Co.* 1936.
Historical Survey of Great Western Engine Sheds, *Oxford Publishing Co., E. T. Lyons,* 1972/4.
What happened to Steam Volume Two, *P. B. Hands,* 1980.
Loco Profile No. 3 GW 4 cylinder 4-6-0s, *B. Reed, Profile Publications Ltd.,* 1972.
BR Steam Motive Power Depots WR, *P. Bolger, Ian Allan,* 1983.